Foreword

In the kaleidoscope of American society, generational shifts are the vibrant colours that continually reshape our nation's landscape. Each generation brings its unique hues, blending the past with the present to create the tapestry of our collective history. It's a dynamic interplay of experiences, values, and aspirations that defines the ever-evolving spirit of America.

In "From Boom to Zoom: Decoding America's Generational Shift," Ethan Winters invites us on a captivating journey through the generations that have shaped and continue to shape our great nation. Through meticulous research, insightful analysis, and a genuine passion for understanding the human stories behind the statistics, Winters unravels the complex threads of America's generational tapestry.

This book is not just a chronological exploration of birth years; it is a profound examination of the forces that have driven each generation's hopes, dreams, and challenges. It is a testament to the power of generational diversity and the resilience of a nation that thrives on change and innovation.

As we delve into the pages of this book, we will encounter the Silent Generation, the Baby Boomers, Generation X, Millennials, Generation Z, and the emerging Generation Alpha. Through their eyes, we witness the post-war rebuilding, the social revolutions, the digital transformations, and the ever-urgent quest for a brighter future.

Winters' writing is more than a reflection of generational identities; it is an invitation to bridge divides and foster understanding. It is a call to recognize the shared values that unite us across generations and to embrace the wisdom that each cohort brings to the table.

I encourage you to embark on this enlightening journey with an open heart and a curious mind. Whether you are a member of a specific generation seeking to understand your place in history or a curious observer of generational dynamics, this book offers profound insights that will leave you enriched and inspired.

In the end, "From Boom to Zoom" is more than a book about generations; it is a celebration of the human spirit and our collective journey towards a brighter future. It is a reminder that, as we navigate the twists and turns of time, we do so together, bound by the common threads of humanity.

Enjoy the voyage through America's generational shift, and may it illuminate your understanding of the rich tapestry of our nation's history.

—Ethan Winters

Table of Contents

Foreword

- Introduction

Chapter 1: The Generational Mosaic

- Understanding Generations and Their Significance
- The Silent Generation: A Foundation of Resilience
- Baby Boomers: The Shapers of Post-War America
- Generation X: The Bridge to the Digital Age
- Millennials: Navigating Change in the Information Era
- Gen Z: Digital Natives and the Future of America

Chapter 2: The Generational Impact on Culture

- Cultural Trends Across Generations
- Music, Art, and Entertainment
- Fashion and Lifestyle
- Values and Beliefs

Chapter 3: Politics and Policy Through the Ages

- The Political Landscape of Each Generation
- Key Political Moments and Movements
- Generational Differences in Political Ideologies
- Voting Patterns and Civic Engagement

Chapter 4: The Economy and Workforce Dynamics

- The Generational Evolution of the American Workplace
- Economic Challenges Faced by Different Generations
- Entrepreneurship and Innovation Across the Ages
- The Future of Work and Technology

Chapter 5: Technology's Role in Generational Shift

- Technological Milestones in Each Generation
- The Digital Divide: Access and Skills
- Social Media and Its Influence
- Privacy and Ethical Considerations

Chapter 6: The Generational Social Contract

- Generational Perspectives on Social Welfare and Healthcare
- Education: A Lifelong Journey
- Retirement and Aging: Challenges and Solutions
- Family Dynamics and Intergenerational Relationships

Chapter 7: Bridging the Generational Divide

- Strategies for Effective Communication Across Generations
- Building Bridges in the Workplace
- Fostering Generational Understanding in Families and Communities
- The Power of Collaboration

Chapter 8: Shaping America's Future

- The Intersection of Generations and Policy
- Opportunities for Unity and Innovation
- Preparing for the Next Generational Wave
- The Vision for America's Future

Conclusion: Decoding the Tapestry of America's Generations

- Reflections on the Generational Journey
- The Ongoing Evolution of American Society
- The Collective Responsibility to Shape Tomorrow

Appendix A: Resources for Further Reading

- Books, Articles, and Websites on Generational Studies

Acknowledgments

- Gratitude to Those Who Contributed to the Book

About the Author

- A Brief Biography of Ethan Winters

Introduction

In the grand theatre of history, generations emerge as the leading characters, each playing its unique role in shaping the destiny of nations. These generational dynamics are like the threads in a tapestry, weaving together the narrative of a society's evolution. America, a nation defined by its dynamism and diversity, is no exception to this timeless truth. In fact, the story of America is intrinsically tied to its generations.

As we embark on this enlightening journey through "From Boom to Zoom: Decoding America's Generational Shift," we find ourselves at a critical juncture—a crossroads where the past, present, and future intersect. In these pages, we will unravel the intricate tapestry of American society, woven together by the experiences, beliefs, and aspirations of generations spanning nearly a century.

Generations, it turns out, are not just demarcations of age; they are profound forces that influence culture, politics, economics, and technology. Each cohort brings its unique perspective, values, and attitudes to the forefront, leaving an indelible mark on the nation's trajectory. From the stoic resilience of the Silent Generation to the tech-savvy prowess of Generation Z, each generation contributes to the rich mosaic that is America.

In the chapters that follow, we will embark on a historical journey, exploring the generations that have defined America's past and continue to shape its present. We will delve into the Silent Generation, who weathered the storms of the early 20th century, emerging as beacons of resilience during the Great Depression and World War II. The Baby Boomers, born in the post-war era, have wielded their influence over politics, culture, and the workforce for decades. Generation X, often dubbed the bridge between analog and digital worlds, provides a unique lens through which to view the American experience. Millennials, raised in the information age, are now at the forefront of navigating an uncertain future. Finally, Generation Z, the first true digital natives, is poised to redefine the very fabric of American society.

Yet, this book is far more than a historical exposition. It's a profound exploration of how each generation's impact reverberates through culture, politics, the economy, and society at large. It delves deep into the music, art, fashion, and values that have shaped our collective consciousness. It unpacks the political ideologies influenced by generational experiences and examines how these perspectives have evolved. It scrutinises how the economy and the workforce have transformed in response to each generation's unique characteristics. It scrutinises the role of technology, exposing the digital divide that separates generations. It sheds light on the social contracts forged by generations and how they have shaped our education, healthcare, and retirement systems.

But beyond analysis, this book is a call to action. It invites us to recognize the generational divides that exist and challenges us to bridge them with understanding, empathy, and collaboration. It calls on us to seek common ground, harnessing the collective wisdom of the past and leveraging the innovation of the present to sculpt a brighter future for all.

Together, we will decode the generational shift currently underway and chart a course toward a united, innovative, and resilient America. The generations that preceded us have paved the way, and it is our collective responsibility to ensure that the generations that follow inherit a nation enriched by its diversity and bound by its shared values.

So, join me as we embark on this enlightening journey through America's generational landscape. Together, we will navigate the currents of the past, explore the terrain of the present, and chart a course for a better future—a future where generations unite and thrive.

Welcome to "From Boom to Zoom."

—Ethan Winters

Chapter 1: The Generational Mosaic

Understanding Generations and Their Significance

Generations, like the seasons of the year, follow a natural cycle, each with its unique attributes and characteristics. Just as spring gives way to summer, and summer to autumn, generations too evolve, shaping the landscape of their time. They are not static entities but living forces, influenced by the events and cultural currents that sweep through their formative years.

But what exactly defines a generation? In essence, a generation is a cohort of individuals who share a common birth period and, as a result, have been exposed to similar historical, cultural, and social influences during their formative years. This shared experience is the crucible in which the values, attitudes, and behaviours of each generation are forged.

To truly comprehend the significance of generations, we must recognize that they are not mere groupings based on birth years; they are lenses through which we can observe the world. These lenses offer unique perspectives on the challenges and opportunities of their time. They shape the aspirations and ambitions of individuals and influence the collective consciousness of society.

Generations are not monolithic; they are nuanced and diverse. Within each generation, there are subcultures, counter-cultures, and individuals with their own unique experiences. However, overarching themes and shared experiences often emerge, providing insight into the generational character.

The significance of generations lies in their impact on society. They are the architects of cultural change, the driving force behind political movements, and the creators of economic trends. They mould the contours of technological advancement and contribute to the evolution of social norms. In essence, generations are the threads that weave the fabric of our shared history.

As we explore the generations that have defined and continue to define America, we'll uncover the rich tapestry of experiences, beliefs, and values that have shaped their journeys. We'll witness how each generation has left an indelible mark on the nation's history, contributing to the ever-evolving story of America.

But this is not just a historical journey; it's a voyage into the heart of our present and future. By understanding the significance of each generation, we can decode the complexities of our society today and, in doing so, prepare ourselves for the challenges and opportunities that lie ahead.

In the chapters that follow, we will delve into the Silent Generation, Baby Boomers, Generation X, Millennials, and Generation Z. We will unveil their unique stories, exploring the events and cultural phenomena that have defined their lives. As we navigate this generational landscape, keep in mind that each generation is a piece of the puzzle, contributing to the mosaic of America's past, present, and future.

So, dear reader, as we embark on this journey of discovery, let us embrace the power of generations. Let us explore the fascinating tapestry they create and recognize the profound significance of understanding their role in shaping America's destiny.

The Silent Generation: A Foundation of Resilience

In the annals of American history, the Silent Generation occupies a unique space—a generation marked by the fortitude and quiet determination that defined their coming of age during the tumultuous mid-20th century. Born between 1928 and 1945, the Silent Generation is often sandwiched between the more renowned generations, the Greatest Generation and the Baby Boomers. However, their impact on American society is undeniable and forms the foundation of the generational landscape we explore today.

The Silent Generation came of age in the shadow of the Great Depression and the horrors of World War II. Their formative years were defined by scarcity, sacrifice, and a collective will to rebuild a world torn apart by global conflict. As a result, they learned resilience from a young age. Economic hardship and the need for collective action against a common enemy instilled in them a sense of duty, community, and a strong work ethic.

Silent Generation members are often characterised by their commitment to traditional values, strong family bonds, and a sense of responsibility to their communities. They are the stoic survivors of an era marked by economic hardship, political upheaval, and social change. Their nickname, the "Silent Generation," derives from their reputation for being cautious, conventional, and less inclined to rebel against authority.

One of the defining attributes of the Silent Generation is their ability to adapt and endure in the face of adversity. They witnessed the dawn of the nuclear age, the rise of the civil rights movement, and the rapid technological advancements that transformed the world. Through it all, they remained resilient, providing the steady foundation upon which future generations would build.

In the realm of politics, the Silent Generation played a pivotal role in shaping the postwar United States. They were the architects of the Civil Rights Act and the Voting Rights Act, championing civil rights and social justice. Their collective efforts helped lay the groundwork for the monumental changes that would later sweep the nation.

Economically, the Silent Generation witnessed the transition from an industrial to a post-industrial society. They navigated through the challenges of economic recessions and inflation while embracing the opportunities presented by the burgeoning technology and service sectors. Their work ethic and commitment to fiscal responsibility would influence the economic policies of the generations that followed.

In family life, the Silent Generation established the traditional nuclear family model, valuing stability and providing a nurturing environment for their Baby Boomer children. Their values of loyalty, duty, and hard work have been passed down through the generations, influencing the way families interact and support one another.

As we delve into the experiences and impact of the Silent Generation, we'll come to appreciate the resilience, dedication, and sense of duty that define them. Their story is not just one of survival but of thriving in the face of adversity—a story that has left an indelible mark on the America we know today.

In the chapters ahead, we will continue our exploration of generations, moving from the Silent Generation to the Baby Boomers, Generation X, Millennials, and Generation Z. Together, we'll uncover how each generation's unique experiences have shaped the cultural, political, economic, and technological landscape of America.

So, let us continue our journey through the generational tapestry of America, starting with the foundation of resilience provided by the Silent Generation.

Baby Boomers: The Shapers of Post-War America

The post-World War II era in America bore witness to an extraordinary phenomenon—the Baby Boom. A surge in births, beginning in 1946 and lasting until 1964, saw the population of the United States swell by tens of millions. This generation, aptly named the Baby Boomers, would go on to become one of the most influential and transformative cohorts in the nation's history.

Born into an era of economic prosperity and rebuilding, Baby Boomers were raised in a world shaped by the sacrifices and optimism of the Greatest Generation. They emerged as a generation marked by a profound sense of possibility—a generation that would leave an indelible mark on the cultural, political, and economic landscape of America.

The Baby Boomers came of age during the 1960s and 1970s, a time of immense social change and cultural upheaval. They were at the forefront of the civil rights movement, the anti-war protests, and the rise of the counterculture. Their activism and idealism would play a pivotal role in reshaping American society, challenging long-held norms, and pushing for greater social justice.

In politics, the Baby Boomers have left an indelible mark. They witnessed the assassinations of prominent leaders, the Civil Rights Movement, and the protests against the Vietnam War. These experiences fueled their desire for change, and many Baby Boomers became active participants in the political landscape. They would later occupy positions of power, shaping policies and driving significant social and economic reforms.

Economically, the Baby Boomers have influenced various facets of American life. They experienced the economic boom of the post-war years, contributing to the growth of suburbia, the rise of consumer culture, and the expansion of educational opportunities. As they entered the workforce, they played a pivotal role in shaping corporate America and the technological advancements of the late 20th century.

The Baby Boomer generation is also known for redefining traditional family dynamics. They questioned and challenged conventional norms, contributing to shifts in gender roles, family structures, and social expectations. Their experiences as parents and grandparents have influenced parenting styles, education, and the way family relationships are navigated.

In many ways, the Baby Boomers' impact on America is a reflection of their generational spirit—an unyielding belief in the power of change and a commitment to shaping the world around them. They have navigated through tumultuous times, adapting to shifting social, political, and technological landscapes.

As we delve into the experiences and influence of the Baby Boomer generation, we'll gain insight into their role as both beneficiaries and architects of post-war America. Their story is one of transformation, activism, and a determination to leave a lasting legacy.

In the chapters to come, we will continue our exploration of generations, moving from the Baby Boomers to Generation X, Millennials, and Generation Z. Together, we'll uncover how each generation's unique experiences have shaped the cultural, political, economic, and technological landscape of America.

So, let us journey onward through the generational tapestry of America, starting with the Baby Boomers, the shapers of post-war America.

Generation X: The Bridge to the Digital Age

Between the towering presence of the Baby Boomers and the digital natives of Generation Z lies a generation that often operates in the shadows, yet its impact on America's trajectory has been profound. Born roughly between the early 1960s and the late 1970s, Generation X finds itself positioned as a bridge—a connector between the analog past and the digital future.

Growing up during a time of rapid technological advancement, Gen Xers witnessed the emergence of personal computers, the birth of the internet, and the dawn of the digital age. These experiences have shaped their worldview and positioned them as a generation with a unique perspective on the world.

Unlike the Baby Boomers, who navigated through the social and political upheavals of the 1960s and 1970s, Generation X found itself entering adulthood in a world marked by economic recession, global changes, and shifting cultural dynamics. This generation became known for its independent spirit, resilience, and adaptability in the face of uncertainty.

One defining characteristic of Generation X is their embrace of technology. They are often regarded as the first generation to truly straddle the divide between analog and digital worlds. While they grew up with analog technology like cassette tapes and VHS, they quickly adapted to the digital revolution, becoming early adopters of personal computers and the World Wide Web.

Politically, Generation X came of age in a time marked by geopolitical shifts, the end of the Cold War, and the emergence of new global challenges. Their pragmatism and scepticism towards traditional institutions have influenced their approach to politics, leading them to value self-reliance and adaptability.

Economically, Gen Xers faced the challenges of an ever-evolving job market. They were part of the workforce during the rise of the gig economy, witnessing the shift from job security to job flexibility. This experience has had a lasting impact on their approach to work and career choices.

In the realm of culture, Generation X contributed to the alternative music scene, the grunge movement, and a broader shift away from traditional values. Their unique cultural perspective has left an enduring mark on music, film, and literature.

As parents, Generation X faced the challenge of balancing work and family life. They pioneered new approaches to parenting, emphasising quality time with their children and nurturing strong family bonds.

In many ways, Generation X serves as a bridge between the past and the future, carrying the lessons of previous generations into the digital age. Their adaptability, scepticism, and technological prowess have positioned them as a generation of innovators and change-makers.

As we delve into the experiences and impact of Generation X, we'll uncover their role as trailblazers in the digital revolution, their unique approach to politics and economics, and their contributions to the evolving cultural landscape of America.

In the chapters to come, we will continue our exploration of generations, moving from Generation X to Millennials, Generation Z, and beyond. Together, we'll gain a deeper understanding of how each generation's distinctive experiences have shaped the cultural, political, economic, and technological fabric of America.

So, let us continue our journey through the generational tapestry of America, guided by Generation X, the bridge to the digital age.

Millennials: Navigating Change in the Information Era

In the ever-evolving narrative of American generations, one cohort has emerged as both torchbearers of change and inheritors of the digital age—the Millennials. Born roughly between the early 1980s and the mid-1990s, this generation found itself navigating the complexities of a world in flux, marked by unprecedented technological advancements and a rapidly shifting cultural landscape.

Millennials, often referred to as Generation Y, are the first generation to come of age in the Information Era—a time characterised by the proliferation of the internet, the rise of social media, and the democratisation of knowledge. Their lives have been intrinsically intertwined with technology, influencing not only how they communicate and connect but also how they perceive and engage with the world.

As digital natives, Millennials have embraced technology as an integral part of their lives. They were the first to experience the transformational power of the internet, the ubiquity of smartphones, and the advent of social networking platforms. These technological tools have redefined the way they interact with one another, consume information, and engage in the world of work.

The Millennial generation grew up in a world marked by rapid globalisation and the interconnectedness of cultures, economies, and ideas. They witnessed the fall of the Berlin Wall, the spread of the European Union, and the challenges posed by climate change. These global dynamics have informed their worldview and spurred a sense of collective responsibility.

Politically, Millennials have been agents of change. They were at the forefront of the Arab Spring, Occupy Wall Street, and the push for LGBTQ+ rights. Their activism and civic engagement have reshaped political discourse and influenced electoral outcomes. This generation's commitment to social justice, equality, and environmental sustainability is a defining characteristic.

Economically, Millennials came of age during a period marked by financial crises, economic recessions, and evolving workforce dynamics. They navigated the challenges of student debt, job market uncertainty, and the gig economy. As a result, they have adapted to a fast-paced, entrepreneurial approach to work and life.

In the realm of culture, Millennials have influenced trends in fashion, music, and entertainment. They are responsible for the rise of digital streaming platforms, the resurgence of vinyl records, and the popularity of online content creation. Their cultural contributions reflect their preference for authenticity, diversity, and individual expression.

As parents and caregivers, Millennials have challenged traditional parenting norms, emphasising work-life balance, co-parenting, and the use of technology to enhance parenting experiences. They are redefining family dynamics and reshaping the concept of work-life integration.

As we delve into the experiences and impact of the Millennial generation, we'll gain insight into their role as trailblazers of the digital age, their commitment to social and political change, and their unique approach to economics, culture, and family life.

In the chapters to come, we will continue our exploration of generations, moving from Millennials to Generation Z and beyond. Together, we'll unravel the threads of generational influence that shape the cultural, political, economic, and technological fabric of America.

So, let us embark on this journey through the generational tapestry of America, guided by the Millennials, who navigate change in the Information Era.

Gen Z: Digital Natives and the Future of America

In the unfolding narrative of American generations, a new chapter is being written by those who came of age in the 21st century—the digital natives known as Generation Z, or Gen Z for short. Born from the late 1990s to the early 2010s, this cohort is the first to grow up in a world where technology, connectivity, and information are omnipresent. Their experiences and perspectives are charting a course for the future of America and the world.

Gen Z stands at the intersection of history, poised to navigate a rapidly changing landscape. They are true digital natives, having never known a world without the internet, smartphones, and social media. These digital tools have not only shaped the way they communicate but have also redefined their understanding of identity, community, and activism.

Technology is not merely a tool for Gen Z; it is an integral part of their lives. They have harnessed the power of social media to champion causes, connect with global communities, and amplify their voices on issues ranging from climate change to social justice. They are digital storytellers, content creators, and agents of change in a hyperconnected world.

Growing up amidst the complexities of a globalised society, Gen Z has witnessed the consequences of environmental degradation, economic inequality, and political polarisation. These challenges have fueled their commitment to social and environmental activism, inspiring movements like the youth-led climate strikes and the fight for racial justice.

Politically, Gen Z is characterised by a desire for transparency, accountability, and systemic change. They have engaged in online activism, mobilising their peers to participate in the democratic process and advocating for policies that reflect their values. Their approach to politics is marked by a pragmatism that seeks innovative solutions to complex problems.

Economically, Gen Z faces a landscape shaped by rapid technological advancements and evolving workforce dynamics. They are entrepreneurial, resourceful, and adaptable, drawn to careers that allow for flexibility and remote work. Their digital literacy and tech-savvy nature position them as key players in the innovation economy.

In the realm of culture, Gen Z has embraced diversity, inclusivity, and individuality. They challenge traditional norms of gender, identity, and expression, fostering a culture that celebrates authenticity and acceptance. Their influence can be seen in the entertainment industry, where they demand diverse representation and content that reflects their lived experiences.

As we delve into the experiences and impact of Generation Z, we'll gain insight into their role as digital pioneers, their commitment to social and environmental causes, and their unique approach to politics, economics, and culture. Their emergence as a generation of change-makers holds the promise of shaping a more inclusive, tech-driven, and interconnected future for America and the world.

In the chapters to come, we will continue our exploration of generations, weaving together the stories of Gen Z with those of their predecessors. Together, we will uncover how each generation's distinctive experiences have shaped the cultural, political, economic, and technological fabric of America.

So, let us embark on this journey through the generational tapestry of America, guided by Generation Z, the digital natives who are shaping the future of our nation.

Chapter 2: The Generational Impact on Culture

Cultural Trends Across Generations

Culture, like a flowing river, is in a constant state of change. It is shaped by the currents of history, the experiences of generations, and the evolving values of society. In this chapter, we dive deep into the cultural trends that have characterised each generation, understanding how they have influenced music, art, entertainment, fashion, and the core values that define their collective identity.

Music

Music, like a time-travelling vessel, carries the emotions, aspirations, and spirit of each generation across the ages. It is a dynamic tapestry woven with the threads of history, culture, and personal experiences. As we explore the cultural trends that have defined each generation through music, we gain insights into the evolution of society's tastes and values.

The Silent Generation found solace in the soothing melodies of crooners like Frank Sinatra and the harmonious sounds of doo-wop groups. The post-war years were marked by a longing for stability and love, and the music of this era resonated with those desires. As society rebuilt itself, the soundtrack was one of nostalgia, romance, and the promise of better days.

Baby Boomers ushered in a musical revolution with the advent of rock 'n' roll. Icons like Elvis Presley and The Beatles became the voices of a generation that was challenging the status quo. The 1960s and 1970s saw the rise of folk and protest music, with artists like Bob Dylan and Joan Baez lending their voices to civil rights and anti-war movements. Music became a powerful tool for social change and self-expression.

Generation X brought punk, new wave, and alternative rock to the forefront. This generation's music was marked by a sense of cynicism and disillusionment, mirroring the political and economic uncertainties of the 1980s and 1990s. Bands like The Clash, The Police, and Nirvana embodied the counterculture spirit, questioning traditional norms and the establishment.

For **Millennials**, the digital age brought about a democratisation of music. The rise of the internet and streaming platforms allowed for a diverse array of genres and artists to thrive. Hip-hop, pop-punk, and electronic dance music became defining genres, reflecting the multicultural, tech-savvy nature of this generation. Music became not only a form of entertainment but also a means of self-discovery and empowerment.

Generation Z, with their limitless access to music through streaming services and social media, are shaping the future of music consumption. They champion artists who speak to their values of inclusivity, activism, and authenticity. Gen Z's musical tastes span multiple genres, reflecting their diverse and globalised perspective. Music is not just a form of expression for them; it is a platform for advocating change and reflecting their evolving worldview.

In the ever-changing symphony of generational experiences, music remains a constant companion, carrying the emotions and aspirations of each era. It is a mirror reflecting the hopes, dreams, and challenges of generations past and present, and it continues to evolve as new voices emerge to shape the soundtrack of our times.

Art and Entertainment

Art and entertainment are the canvases upon which generations paint their values, desires, and visions of the world. From classic masterpieces to contemporary blockbusters, these cultural expressions reflect the pulse of society and offer a window into the hearts and minds of each generation.

The Silent Generation found solace and inspiration in the world of classic art and the golden age of cinema. Paintings from this era often depicted scenes of idyllic landscapes and the triumph of human spirit. The works of artists like Jackson Pollock and Mark Rothko conveyed the complexities of human emotion through abstract expressionism. In the realm of entertainment, stars like Audrey Hepburn and Cary Grant personified elegance and grace on the silver screen.

Baby Boomers, driven by the counterculture movement, rejected traditional norms and embraced avant-garde art. Pop art, led by artists like Andy Warhol, celebrated the mundane and the commercial, challenging the boundaries of what could be considered art. In the world of entertainment, music festivals like Woodstock became symbols of a cultural revolution, bringing together people in a celebration of music, peace, and freedom.

Generation X gravitated towards gritty and unconventional forms of art, finding beauty in street art and graffiti. Artists like Keith Haring and Jean-Michel Basquiat used the streets as their canvas, reflecting the urban decay and social issues of their time. In cinema, films like "Pulp Fiction" and "Trainspotting" captured the rawness of life in the late 20th century, with their nonlinear narratives and anti-establishment themes.

Millennials, raised in the information age, saw the emergence of internet art and viral sensations. Memes, GIFs, and online communities reshaped how they expressed and consumed culture. In cinema, they embraced epic franchises like Harry Potter and The Lord of the Rings, seeking escapism in fantastical worlds. The rise of digital platforms and content creation also allowed for a new wave of artists and creators to flourish.

Generation Z is pushing the boundaries of art and entertainment in the digital age. Digital art, virtual reality experiences, and online content creation have become prominent mediums for self-expression and storytelling. Gen Z values diversity and representation in media, demanding authenticity and social relevance in the content they consume. Online influencers and social media platforms play a significant role in shaping their artistic and entertainment preferences.

Across the generations, art and entertainment serve as reflections of societal values, expressions of rebellion, and sources of inspiration. They capture the essence of their respective eras and provide a bridge between the past and the future. As technology continues to reshape the way we create and consume culture, the artistic and entertainment landscapes will evolve, offering new forms of expression for generations to come.

Fashion and Lifestyle

Fashion is a language—a visual expression of identity, values, and cultural shifts. Each generation has its own sartorial story, reflecting the times they lived in and the evolving societal norms. Let's take a journey through the fashion trends and lifestyle choices that have shaped the identity of each generation.

The Silent Generation embraced a conservative and formal dress code. This generation's fashion was characterised by tailored suits, modest dresses, and an emphasis on practicality and durability. The post-war years demanded a sense of responsibility and adherence to traditional values, which were mirrored in their attire.

Baby Boomers, fueled by the counterculture movement, rebelled against the formalities of their parents' generation. They adopted tie-dye shirts, bell-bottom pants, and fringe jackets as symbols of freedom and self-expression. The fashion of this era became a reflection of their desire to challenge the status quo and break away from traditional norms.

Generation X introduced grunge fashion, characterised by flannel shirts, ripped jeans, and combat boots. This generation rejected the materialism of the 1980s and 1990s and embraced a more relaxed, anti-establishment style. Their fashion choices mirrored their scepticism towards societal conventions.

Millennials, growing up in the information age, witnessed the rise of fast fashion and a trend towards comfort and convenience. Athleisure wear, characterised by yoga pants and sneakers, became a staple of their wardrobe. This generation's fashion choices reflected the blending of work and leisure in the digital age, as well as a focus on self-care and personal well-being.

Generation Z is redefining fashion and lifestyle choices with a focus on sustainability and individuality. They value eco-friendly fashion, thrift shopping, and mixing and matching styles from different eras. Influenced by online influencers and social media, Gen Z is less bound by traditional gender norms and embraces a broader range of self-expression.

Lifestyle choices are also evolving with each generation. The Silent Generation emphasised stability, community, and family values. They found solace in traditional family structures and believed in the importance of hard work and responsibility.

Baby Boomers ushered in a wave of experimentation and countercultural lifestyles. They challenged traditional gender roles, embraced communal living, and explored alternative forms of spirituality.

Generation X, navigating economic uncertainty and changing family dynamics, sought work-life balance and prioritised self-reliance. They were early adopters of technology and embraced a DIY ethos.

Millennials, raised in the digital age, value experiences over possessions. They prioritise travel, personal growth, and work-life integration. The gig economy and remote work have allowed them to lead more flexible lifestyles.

Generation Z, growing up in a hyperconnected world, places a premium on authenticity and social responsibility. They seek meaningful connections, value diversity, and use technology as a tool for change and activism.

In a world of evolving fashion and lifestyles, each generation's choices are a reflection of their values, aspirations, and the unique challenges they face. As we explore these trends, we gain a deeper understanding of the generational identities that have shaped our culture and society.

Values and Beliefs

Values and beliefs are the compasses that guide individuals and shape the moral and ethical fabric of society. They are deeply influenced by historical events, cultural shifts, and the collective experiences of each generation. Let's explore how values and beliefs have evolved across generations, providing insight into the unique character of each era.

The Silent Generation, marked by their resilience, values loyalty, duty, and community. Growing up during times of economic hardship and war, they developed a strong sense of responsibility to their families and communities. Sacrifice and hard work were virtues instilled in them, and they carried these values into their adult lives.

Baby Boomers came of age during the counterculture movement, embracing values of freedom, individualism, and social justice. They challenged traditional norms and advocated for civil rights, women's rights, and environmental conservation. This generation believed in the power of collective action and used their voices to effect change.

Generation X navigated the uncertainties of the late 20th century, which influenced their values of self-reliance, adaptability, and scepticism. They witnessed political scandals and economic recessions, fostering a pragmatic and independent mindset. This generation often sought solutions outside traditional institutions and valued individualism.

Millennials, raised in the information age, prioritise diversity, inclusivity, and social responsibility. They are global citizens, advocating for equality, sustainability, and technological innovation. Their exposure to a rapidly changing world has instilled in them a sense of adaptability and a desire for work-life balance and personal well-being.

Generation Z, growing up in a hyperconnected world, prioritises authenticity, social justice, and environmental sustainability. They use technology as a tool for change and activism, believing in the power of their voices to shape a better future. Gen Z champions inclusivity and demands accountability from institutions.

These values and beliefs influence not only individual behaviours but also collective actions. They shape political ideologies, social movements, and the ways in which each generation seeks to make a positive impact on the world.

The Silent Generation's values of loyalty and duty were reflected in their commitment to community and family, as well as their resilience during times of crisis. Baby Boomers' values of freedom and social justice fueled the civil rights and environmental movements of their era. Generation X's scepticism led to innovative solutions and alternative approaches to societal challenges.

Millennials' values of inclusivity and sustainability have driven social and environmental initiatives, while Generation Z's values of authenticity and social justice are at the forefront of contemporary activism.

As we explore the values and beliefs of each generation, we gain a deeper understanding of the motivations and ideals that have shaped their actions and decisions. These values are the threads that weave the tapestry of generational identity and continue to influence the world we live in today.

Chapter 3: Politics and Policy Through the Ages

The Political Landscape of Each Generation

Politics is the arena where generations often clash, collaborate, and leave their mark on the course of history. In this chapter, we'll journey through the political landscapes that each generation has navigated, shedding light on the values, ideologies, and key events that have shaped their political identities.

The Silent Generation, born during the aftermath of World War I and the Great Depression, was marked by a sense of duty, loyalty, and collective responsibility. As they entered the political arena, they often aligned with the establishment, valuing stability and continuity. This generation came of age during the early years of the Cold War, influencing their hawkish stance on foreign policy and their support for containment strategies. They played a pivotal role in the civil rights movement, pushing for desegregation and equal rights.

Baby Boomers, the largest generation in U.S. history, emerged as agents of change during the turbulent 1960s and 1970s. Their political landscape was shaped by civil rights activism, anti-war protests, and the women's liberation movement. They challenged authority, questioned traditional norms, and pushed for social justice. The political divisions of this era, particularly regarding the Vietnam War and civil rights legislation, left an indelible mark on their generation. As they aged, some Boomers became part of the political establishment, while others remained steadfast in their commitment to progressive causes.

Generation X, sandwiched between the idealism of the Boomers and the digital age, developed a pragmatic and sceptical approach to politics. They witnessed the Watergate scandal and the economic challenges of the 1970s, fostering a sense of disillusionment with traditional institutions. This generation's political landscape was marked by a shift towards individualism and self-reliance. They were open to innovative approaches to governance and often championed economic conservatism. The end of the Cold War and the fall of the Berlin Wall during their formative years influenced their perspective on international relations.

Millennials, raised in the era of information technology and globalisation, prioritise diversity, inclusivity, and social justice in their political landscape. They are often described as socially liberal and tech-savvy. The 9/11 attacks and the subsequent War on Terror were defining events during their formative years, influencing their views on security and foreign policy. Millennials played a pivotal role in the election of Barack Obama, emphasising the importance of hope and change in their political discourse. They have also been at the forefront of issues such as climate change and LGBTQ+ rights.

Generation Z, the first true digital natives, have come of age in a hyperconnected world that has shaped their political landscape. They value authenticity, social justice, and environmental sustainability. Their political engagement often takes place online, with social media platforms serving as tools for advocacy and mobilisation. Gen Z's stance on issues like gun control, racial equality, and climate change reflects their commitment to effecting change and holding institutions accountable.

The political landscape of each generation is influenced by the unique historical events and cultural shifts they have experienced. The Silent Generation's sense of duty and resilience, Baby Boomers' activism and idealism, Generation X's pragmatism and scepticism, Millennials' focus on social justice and technology, and Generation Z's digital activism all contribute to the complex tapestry of American politics. As we explore the political identities of each generation, we gain a deeper understanding of the forces that have shaped the nation's political landscape and continue to do so in the present day.

Key Political Moments and Movements

Throughout American history, key political moments and movements have left an indelible mark on the nation's trajectory. These moments are often intertwined with generational experiences, shaping the political landscapes of their respective eras. Let's delve into some of the pivotal moments and movements that have defined each generation's engagement with the political realm.

The Silent Generation witnessed the rise of the civil rights movement in the 1950s and 1960s. This was a transformative period characterised by nonviolent protests, boycotts, and acts of civil disobedience. Leaders like Martin Luther King Jr. and Rosa Parks inspired a generation to push for racial equality and the end of segregation. The Civil Rights Act of 1964 and the Voting Rights Act of 1965 were watershed moments that marked significant progress in the fight for civil rights. The Silent Generation played a crucial role in supporting these movements and advocating for justice and equality.

Baby Boomers were at the forefront of the anti-war movement during the Vietnam War era. The war, marked by intense protests and demonstrations, deeply divided the nation. The activism of this generation culminated in events like the Moratorium to End the War in Vietnam and the Kent State shootings. The anti-war movement had a profound impact on public opinion and ultimately contributed to the U.S. withdrawal from Vietnam. Baby Boomers' passion for social justice extended beyond anti-war efforts to include the civil rights and women's liberation movements, making the 1960s and 1970s a time of significant political upheaval and change.

Generation X came of age during the tumultuous political landscape of the late 20th century. The Watergate scandal and subsequent resignation of President Richard Nixon eroded trust in government institutions and fueled a sense of scepticism among this generation. They witnessed the Iran Hostage Crisis and the energy crisis, which added to the prevailing sense of uncertainty. However, the fall of the Berlin Wall in 1989 and the end of the Cold War offered a glimmer of hope and optimism for a more interconnected world. Generation X often approached politics with a pragmatic and independent mindset, seeking innovative solutions to complex challenges.

Millennials came of age in the wake of the 9/11 attacks, which had a profound impact on their political landscape. The subsequent War on Terror, including the invasion of Iraq and Afghanistan, stirred debates about national security and foreign policy. Millennials were also instrumental in the election of Barack Obama in 2008, drawn to his message of hope and change. They played a pivotal role in pushing for marriage equality and LGBTQ+ rights, as well as advocating for action on climate change. The Occupy Wall Street movement, which called for economic reform and greater income equality, also gained momentum during this generation's formative years.

Generation Z has been characterised by a strong focus on social justice and activism. The Black Lives Matter movement, ignited by the killing of Trayvon Martin in 2012 and further fueled by high-profile cases of police brutality, has resonated deeply with this generation. Gen Z has used social media platforms to organise protests, advocate for racial equality, and demand accountability from institutions. They have also been vocal advocates for gun control reform, following events such as the Parkland school shooting in 2018. Climate activism, inspired by figures like Greta Thunberg, has galvanised Gen Z's commitment to environmental sustainability.

These key political moments and movements have not only shaped the values and beliefs of each generation but have also influenced their political engagement. They reflect the broader societal changes and challenges that have defined different eras in American history. As we explore the political landscapes of each generation, it becomes evident how these moments have contributed to the nation's evolving political identity and continue to influence the present-day political discourse.

Generational Differences in Political Ideologies

Politics is the battleground where generational differences often come to the forefront. Each generation carries with it a unique set of political ideologies and priorities that shape their views on governance, social issues, and the role of government. Let's explore the distinct political ideologies that have defined each generation's engagement with the political landscape.

The Silent Generation, born between the mid-1920s and early 1940s, often leaned towards conservative and pragmatic political ideologies. Shaped by the aftermath of the Great Depression and World War II, they embraced values of loyalty, duty, and collective responsibility. This generation tended to be fiscally conservative, prioritising economic stability and the reduction of government debt. Their views on social issues were often more traditional, reflecting the social norms of their time.

Baby Boomers, the generation born between the mid-1940s and mid-1960s, are known for their idealism and activism. They emerged during the tumultuous 1960s and 1970s, which shaped their progressive political ideologies. Baby Boomers were at the forefront of the civil rights movement, the anti-war protests, and the women's liberation movement. They often championed social justice, equal rights, and government intervention in addressing societal inequalities. This generation's political engagement reflected their desire for change and a more equitable society.

Generation X, born from the mid-1960s to the early 1980s, developed a pragmatic and sceptical approach to politics. Growing up during a period of economic uncertainty and political scandals, they tended to be economically conservative and cautious about government intervention. Generation X often sought innovative solutions to governance challenges and was open to market-based reforms. Their scepticism towards traditional institutions and a desire for self-reliance influenced their political ideologies.

Millennials, born from the early 1980s to the mid-1990s, are characterised by their progressive and socially liberal political ideologies. Raised in the information age, they prioritise diversity, inclusivity, and social justice. Millennials have been vocal advocates for issues such as marriage equality, LGBTQ+ rights, and climate change. They often lean towards economic liberalism and government intervention in addressing income inequality and environmental concerns. Their political engagement is heavily influenced by technology and a globalised perspective.

Generation Z, born from the mid-1990s to the early 2010s, have emerged as activists with a strong focus on social justice and environmental sustainability. Their political ideologies are marked by a commitment to authenticity and accountability. Gen Z often leans towards socially liberal positions on issues like racial equality, gender identity, and gun control. They are also ardent advocates for climate action and have used technology to mobilise and amplify their voices in the political arena.

Generational differences in political ideologies are not static but evolve in response to changing societal, economic, and cultural factors. These differences shape the dynamics of American politics, influencing policy debates, election outcomes, and the direction of the nation. Understanding these generational variations in political ideologies is essential for grasping the complexities of the political landscape and the forces that drive political change over time.

Voting Patterns and Civic Engagement

Voting and civic engagement are the lifeblood of a democracy, serving as the means by which individuals participate in shaping the nation's future. These activities are also shaped by generational influences, reflecting the values, priorities, and political ideologies of each generation. Let's delve into the voting patterns and civic engagement habits that have defined each generation.

The Silent Generation, known for their sense of duty and community, has consistently demonstrated high levels of voter turnout throughout their lives. They came of age during a time when civic duty was emphasised, and they have carried that ethos into their voting habits. This generation often prioritises stability and fiscal responsibility, influencing their choices at the ballot box. Their voting patterns have reflected a more conservative and pragmatic approach to governance.

Baby Boomers, characterised by their idealism and activism, have also been active participants in the political process. They were heavily involved in the civil rights movement, anti-war protests, and other social justice causes. Their voting patterns often align with progressive values, reflecting their desire for social change and government intervention in addressing inequalities. As this generation has aged, they have continued to be a significant voting bloc, influencing election outcomes.

Generation X, marked by their scepticism and pragmatism, have shown varying levels of engagement in civic and political activities. They tend to prioritise individualism and self-reliance, which can influence their participation in collective actions like voting. However, Generation X has often sought innovative ways to engage with politics, such as supporting third-party candidates and advocating for market-based reforms. Their voting patterns reflect a pragmatic approach to governance.

Millennials, raised in the digital age and motivated by social justice causes, have shown a strong interest in civic engagement. They are known for their enthusiasm in supporting candidates who align with their progressive values. However, their voting patterns have been marked by lower turnout rates in some elections. Nevertheless, they have been instrumental in driving political change, particularly in advocating for issues such as marriage equality, climate action, and economic reform. Millennials' use of technology and social media has also reshaped the way they engage with politics, making them vocal advocates and organisers in the digital realm.

Generation Z, the first true digital natives, have embraced technology as a tool for civic engagement. They are often characterised by their activism and commitment to social justice causes. Gen Z's voting patterns are still emerging as they come of age, but their engagement in issues like gun control, racial equality, and climate change has been remarkable. They use social media platforms to organise protests, advocate for change, and mobilise their peers. Gen Z's voting patterns are expected to reflect their progressive values and commitment to making a positive impact on society.

Understanding the voting patterns and civic engagement habits of each generation provides valuable insights into the dynamics of American politics. These habits are influenced by a complex interplay of generational experiences, values, and cultural factors. As each generation continues to evolve and engage with the political process, their impact on the nation's political landscape will shape the direction of the country for years to come.

Chapter 4: The Economy and Workforce Dynamics

The Generational Evolution of the American Workplace

The American workplace has undergone significant transformations over the years, driven by technological advancements, societal shifts, and the evolving expectations of each generation. In this chapter, we'll explore how the American workplace has evolved in response to the unique characteristics and preferences of each generation.

The Silent Generation, born during the Great Depression and World War II, entered the workforce during a time of economic recovery and rebuilding. They were known for their loyalty, discipline, and work ethic. The workplaces of the Silent Generation were often characterised by hierarchical structures and long-term job security. Company loyalty was paramount, and employees often stayed with the same organisation for decades. This generation's commitment to their careers and strong work ethic laid the foundation for the post-war economic boom.

Baby Boomers, the generation that followed, entered the workforce during a period of immense social change and economic growth. They challenged traditional workplace norms and sought more autonomy and self-expression. The 1960s and 1970s saw the rise of the "white-collar" worker, and Baby Boomers embraced the concept of work-life balance. This generation played a significant role in advancing women's rights and diversity in the workplace. The workplace of Baby Boomers reflected their values of individualism and self-fulfilment.

Generation X, sandwiched between the idealism of the Boomers and the digital age, navigated a changing economic landscape marked by recessions and corporate downsizing. They sought job security but were often confronted with a sense of impermanence. Generation X valued adaptability and embraced technology, which transformed the workplace. The concept of remote work and flexible schedules began to gain traction during this era. Gen Xers were often described as the first "latchkey kids," experiencing both parents in the workforce and gaining a sense of self-reliance.

Millennials, raised in the information age, have redefined the American workplace. They prioritise work-life balance, personal fulfilment, and opportunities for professional growth. Millennials have been instrumental in shaping the concept of the "gig economy," seeking flexibility and independence in their careers. This generation's familiarity with technology has accelerated remote work and digital collaboration, transforming traditional office dynamics. They have also advocated for diversity and inclusion in the workplace, challenging traditional hierarchies.

Generation Z, the first true digital natives, have entered the workforce with a focus on authenticity and innovation. They value purpose-driven work and are drawn to organisations that align with their values. Gen Z's technological prowess has further accelerated remote work and digital communication. This generation also values diversity and social responsibility in the workplace, advocating for sustainable practices and ethical business conduct. Their arrival in the workforce has spurred discussions about the future of work, including the potential impact of artificial intelligence and automation.

The American workplace continues to evolve, shaped by the values, expectations, and technological advancements of each generation. Understanding these generational dynamics is essential for organisations seeking to attract, retain, and engage a diverse workforce. As we explore the generational evolution of the American workplace, we gain insights into the changing nature of work and the opportunities and challenges it presents in the 21st century.

Economic Challenges Faced by Different Generations

The economic landscape has been a defining factor in the lives of different generations, shaping their financial opportunities and challenges. In this chapter, we'll explore the distinct economic hurdles that each generation has faced as they navigated their careers and financial futures.

The Silent Generation, born during the Great Depression and coming of age during World War II, experienced economic instability early in life. This generation learned the values of thriftiness, savings, and frugality from their parents, who had weathered the hardships of the Depression. Despite facing economic adversity, they were often characterised by their commitment to job security and long-term employment. The workplace of the Silent Generation provided opportunities for career longevity, but it was also marked by gender and racial disparities.

Baby Boomers, born during the postwar economic boom, enjoyed greater economic prosperity during their formative years. They benefited from the expansion of higher education opportunities and entered the workforce during a period of job growth and rising incomes. However, the economic challenges for Baby Boomers emerged as they aged. Many faced the burden of high-interest mortgages, and the 1970s energy crisis and stagflation created economic uncertainties. Additionally, the looming challenges of funding retirement became a growing concern as this generation aged.

Generation X, sandwiched between the Boomers and the digital age, faced economic challenges marked by recessions and corporate downsizing. They were the first generation to witness the rise of dual-income households, often with both parents in the workforce. While this brought economic stability to some, it also meant increased work demands and the need for work-life balance. Gen Xers experienced the advent of technology, which transformed industries and job requirements. They adapted to an era of job mobility and embraced a more pragmatic approach to career advancement.

Millennials, raised in the digital age, entered the workforce during the Great Recession of 2008. They faced a job market marked by high student loan debt and a shortage of entry-level positions. This generation witnessed the gig economy's rise, characterised by short-term contracts and freelancing, which offered flexibility but often lacked job security and benefits. Millennials also faced housing affordability challenges, with rising rents and home prices outpacing income growth. Saving for retirement became a more daunting task as traditional pension plans faded away.

Generation Z, the first true digital natives, entered the workforce with a focus on innovation and adaptability. They grappled with the economic consequences of the COVID-19 pandemic, which disrupted traditional work patterns and heightened the importance of remote work and digital skills. Gen Zers often balance the demands of education with part-time jobs and gig work to cover rising tuition costs and living expenses. They face economic challenges related to income inequality and the high cost of living in urban areas.

Understanding the economic challenges faced by each generation provides valuable insights into their financial perspectives, career choices, and priorities. These challenges are shaped by a complex interplay of historical events, technological advancements, and societal shifts. As each generation continues to navigate the economic landscape, their experiences contribute to ongoing discussions about financial security, retirement planning, and the future of work.

Entrepreneurship and Innovation Across the Ages

Entrepreneurship and innovation are driving forces of economic growth and cultural change. Each generation has contributed its own entrepreneurial spirit and innovative ideas, shaping industries and transforming the way we live and work. In this chapter, we'll explore the entrepreneurial journeys and innovative contributions of different generations.

The Silent Generation, born during the Great Depression and raised in an era of economic hardship, often prioritised stability and job security. However, many members of this generation went on to become successful entrepreneurs and innovators. They founded businesses that contributed to the post-war economic boom. The Silent Generation's innovations spanned industries, from technology and manufacturing to healthcare and finance. Their work ethic and commitment to quality played a significant role in shaping the business landscape.

Baby Boomers, known for their idealism and activism, brought an entrepreneurial spirit to the 1960s and 1970s. Many Boomers founded businesses that reflected their values and ideals. The counterculture movement inspired innovative approaches to music, fashion, and lifestyle, leading to the rise of new industries. Baby Boomers also played a pivotal role in the technology revolution, contributing to the development of personal computing and the internet. Their entrepreneurial ventures transformed the way we communicate and access information.

Generation X, navigating the economic uncertainties of the late 20th century, embraced innovation as a means of survival. They founded startups and technology companies that challenged traditional business models. Generation X entrepreneurs were early adopters of the internet, paving the way for e-commerce and the digital age. Their innovations in software, gaming, and telecommunications laid the groundwork for the interconnected world we live in today. Gen X's entrepreneurial mindset emphasised adaptability and creative problem-solving.

Millennials, raised in the information age, have redefined entrepreneurship and innovation. They are known for their tech-savvy approach to business and their ability to disrupt traditional industries. Millennials founded startups that leveraged the sharing economy, changing the way we travel, shop, and work. They prioritised social impact and sustainability, leading to innovations in renewable energy, sustainable fashion, and ethical consumerism. Millennials' digital acumen has reshaped marketing and communication, influencing the way businesses connect with consumers.

Generation Z, the first true digital natives, have embraced entrepreneurship and innovation from a young age. They are characterised by their ability to harness technology for creative ventures. Gen Z entrepreneurs have leveraged social media platforms to launch e-commerce businesses, personal brands, and online content ventures. Their innovations extend to areas like artificial intelligence, virtual reality, and blockchain technology. Gen Z's commitment to authenticity and social responsibility drives entrepreneurial ventures that prioritise ethical business practices and social impact.

The entrepreneurial and innovative spirit of each generation has left an indelible mark on the business landscape. These contributions have not only shaped industries but have also influenced societal values and cultural trends. As we explore the entrepreneurial journeys and innovative achievements of different generations, we gain a deeper understanding of the evolving business landscape and the impact of innovation on our lives.

The Future of Work and Technology

The nexus of work and technology is at the heart of the ongoing transformation of the American economy and the global landscape. The confluence of automation, artificial intelligence, and digital connectivity is reshaping industries, job roles, and the very nature of work itself. In this chapter, we'll explore how different generations are experiencing and shaping the future of work and technology.

The Silent Generation, born during a time of economic hardship and world wars, witnessed the advent of computers and early forms of automation. They saw the evolution of mainframe computers and the birth of the internet. While many of them may not have directly engaged with these technologies in their careers, they played pivotal roles in adapting traditional industries to the digital age. Their work ethic and commitment to quality contributed to the development of technology-driven business practices.

Baby Boomers, as they entered the workforce, experienced the emergence of personal computing and the internet. They played a significant role in driving the adoption of technology in various sectors, from finance and healthcare to education and entertainment. Baby Boomers were among the first to explore the potential of e-commerce and digital marketing. Their leadership positions within organisations often involved implementing technological innovations and adapting to changing business landscapes.

Generation X, as digital natives, were early adopters of personal technology devices and witnessed the rise of the World Wide Web. They played a pivotal role in the dot-com boom and the subsequent tech bubble burst. Generation X professionals often found themselves at the forefront of the digital revolution, navigating the challenges and opportunities of a rapidly evolving tech landscape. They embraced remote work and digital communication tools, setting the stage for future work trends.

Millennials, born into the information age, have been at the forefront of the gig economy and the rise of remote work. They have championed the use of technology for collaboration, communication, and entrepreneurship. Millennials are known for their proficiency in digital marketing, social media, and e-commerce. Their values of work-life balance and personal fulfilment have reshaped workplace norms and expectations, driving the demand for flexible work arrangements and remote job opportunities.

Generation Z, the first true digital natives, are poised to shape the future of work and technology. They have grown up in a hyperconnected world and are fluent in the use of technology for both personal and professional purposes. Gen Z's entrepreneurial spirit, combined with their technological prowess, is driving innovation in fields such as artificial intelligence, virtual reality, and blockchain technology. They are likely to continue pushing for remote work options and flexible job arrangements.

The future of work and technology is dynamic and continually evolving, with each generation contributing to its development. Automation and artificial intelligence will continue to impact the workforce, leading to the creation of new jobs and the transformation of existing ones. The way we collaborate, communicate, and conduct business will also undergo further changes, shaped by the evolving expectations and values of each generation.

As we explore the future of work and technology, we gain insights into the opportunities and challenges that lie ahead and the ways in which different generations are navigating this rapidly changing landscape.

Chapter 5: Technology's Role in Generational Shift

Technological Milestones in Each Generation

Technological innovation has been a driving force in shaping the experiences and worldviews of different generations. Each generation has witnessed the emergence of groundbreaking technologies that have transformed society, redefined communication, and revolutionised industries. In this chapter, we'll explore the technological milestones that have left an indelible mark on each generation.

The Silent Generation, born during a time of economic hardship and world wars, saw the rise of several transformative technologies. The development of the first commercially successful computer, the UNIVAC, in the early 1950s marked a significant milestone. This generation also witnessed the birth of the internet's predecessor, ARPANET, in the late 1960s. While they may not have personally interacted with these early computing technologies, their contributions to science and industry laid the foundation for the digital age.

Baby Boomers, who came of age during the cultural revolution of the 1960s and 1970s, witnessed the rapid advancement of personal computing. The introduction of the microprocessor in the early 1970s paved the way for the first generation of personal computers, such as the Altair 8800 and the Apple II. Boomers embraced these innovations, fueling the home computer revolution. Additionally, the launch of the IBM PC in 1981 marked a pivotal moment in the history of personal computing, ushering in the era of desktop computing.

Generation X, growing up in the 1980s and 1990s, experienced the proliferation of the internet and the birth of the World Wide Web. The development of the World Wide Web by Sir Tim Berners-Lee in 1990 revolutionised information access and communication. The popularisation of email and the emergence of the first web browsers, including Mosaic and Netscape Navigator, transformed the way people connected and obtained information. Gen Xers were early adopters of these technologies, paving the way for the digital communication era.

Millennials, raised in the information age, were witness to the rapid evolution of mobile technology and social media. The launch of the first iPhone in 2007 marked a game-changing moment, bringing the internet and communication tools to people's pockets. Millennials were at the forefront of social media platforms like Facebook, Twitter, and Instagram, reshaping the way society communicates, shares information, and builds online communities. Additionally, the growth of cloud computing and the rise of streaming services revolutionised the way we access and consume media.

Generation Z, the first true digital natives, have experienced a hyperconnected world characterised by the proliferation of smartphones, smart devices, and artificial intelligence. The advent of virtual reality (VR) and augmented reality (AR) technologies has expanded the possibilities of immersive experiences and entertainment. Gen Zers have grown up with on-demand streaming services, AI-powered virtual assistants, and the Internet of Things (IoT). They are likely to continue driving innovations in fields like AI, renewable energy, and sustainable technology.

These technological milestones have not only shaped the way generations live and work but have also influenced their cultural values, communication styles, and career choices. As we explore these milestones in each generation, we gain a deeper understanding of the profound impact that technology has had on the world and the generations that have contributed to its evolution.

The Digital Divide: Access and Skills

In the digital age, access to technology and digital skills are defining factors that shape opportunities and participation in the modern world. The digital divide, often described as the gap between those who have access to technology and those who do not, has significant implications for different generations. In this chapter, we'll explore how access to technology and digital skills have evolved and impacted each generation.

The Silent Generation, born during a time of economic hardship and world wars, did not grow up with digital technology. Their early years were marked by limited access to technology, which was primarily reserved for scientific and military purposes. As they entered the workforce, the advent of early computing systems presented both opportunities and challenges. Many members of the Silent Generation had to adapt to new technologies as they became more prevalent in the workplace. Their ability to embrace these changes often depended on their willingness to learn and adapt.

Baby Boomers, who came of age during the 1960s and 1970s, witnessed the emergence of personal computing but had to learn these technologies later in life. They often experienced a digital divide in terms of access and skills, with younger Boomers being more tech-savvy than their older counterparts. The adoption of personal computers and the internet was not uniform across this generation, and many had to acquire digital skills through training and self-learning as technology evolved.

Generation X, growing up in the 1980s and 1990s, straddled the transition from analog to digital technologies. They were among the first to embrace personal computing and the internet during their formative years. However, access to technology and digital skills varied based on socioeconomic factors. Gen Xers who had early exposure to computers and the internet often developed advanced digital skills, while others had to catch up as these technologies became more integral to work and daily life.

Millennials, raised in the information age, were the first generation to come of age with widespread access to digital technology. They experienced the digital divide in terms of access to high-speed internet and advanced devices. Rural and underserved communities often faced challenges in terms of broadband access and digital infrastructure. However, the digital skills of Millennials were generally more advanced than previous generations, as they grew up in an environment that encouraged digital literacy.

Generation Z, the first true digital natives, have been raised in a hyperconnected world. They have had early access to smartphones, tablets, and high-speed internet from a young age. The digital divide for Gen Z often revolves around issues of digital privacy, cybersecurity, and responsible technology use. While they possess innate digital skills, they also face unique challenges related to online safety and the responsible use of technology.

The digital divide is not just about access to technology but also about the ability to leverage digital tools effectively. It is a complex issue influenced by factors such as socioeconomic status, geography, and educational opportunities. Addressing the digital divide is essential for ensuring equal access to educational, economic, and social opportunities for all generations. As we explore the impact of the digital divide on different generations, we gain insights into the evolving role of technology in society and the need for equitable access and digital literacy for all.

Social Media and Its Influence

The rise of social media has been one of the most transformative phenomena of the digital age, reshaping the way people communicate, connect, and express themselves. Social media platforms have influenced cultural trends, political movements, and the very fabric of society. In this chapter, we'll explore how social media has evolved and its impact on different generations.

The Silent Generation, born during a time of economic hardship and world wars, did not grow up with social media. They often experienced its emergence later in life, and their use of social media tends to be less frequent compared to younger generations. However, many Silents have found value in social media for connecting with family and friends, sharing memories, and staying informed about current events. They appreciate the convenience of digital communication but may approach it with caution.

Baby Boomers, who came of age during the 1960s and 1970s, were among the first to embrace social media as it gained popularity in the 2000s. They use platforms like Facebook and LinkedIn to reconnect with old friends, share family updates, and engage in professional networking. Boomers have also utilised social media for political activism and staying informed about social issues. Their presence on social media has expanded over the years, reflecting its growing influence in their lives.

Generation X, growing up in the 1980s and 1990s, were early adopters of social media, witnessing its evolution from platforms like Friendster and MySpace to the dominant presence of Facebook and Twitter. They use social media for a variety of purposes, from connecting with friends and family to accessing news and entertainment. Gen Xers appreciate the convenience of online communication but often maintain a level of privacy and scepticism, given their formative years in a pre-digital world.

Millennials, raised in the information age, have fully embraced social media as an integral part of their lives. They are active on multiple platforms, including Instagram, Snapchat, and TikTok. Social media has become a primary means of communication, self-expression, and networking for Millennials. They use it to connect with peers, share experiences, and advocate for social causes. Millennials have also harnessed social media for professional purposes, using platforms like LinkedIn to advance their careers.

Generation Z, the first true digital natives, have grown up with social media as an essential aspect of their daily lives. They are fluent in platforms like Instagram, Snapchat, and Twitter, and often use social media to curate their online personas and connect with a global audience. Gen Zers are known for their social activism and often use social media as a powerful tool for advocacy and awareness. They value authenticity and are cautious about their digital footprint, actively managing their online presence.

Social media's influence extends beyond individual use; it has played a pivotal role in shaping cultural trends, political movements, and consumer behaviour. It has amplified voices, connected communities, and accelerated the spread of information and ideas. Understanding how different generations engage with and are influenced by social media provides valuable insights into the evolving nature of communication and the role of technology in shaping society.

Privacy and Ethical Considerations

As technology has advanced and digital communication has become ubiquitous, privacy and ethical considerations have taken centre stage in the discourse surrounding the use of technology and the internet. These concerns have evolved in response to changing digital landscapes and have varying implications for different generations. In this chapter, we'll explore the evolving landscape of privacy and ethical considerations and its impact on different generations.

The Silent Generation, born during a time of economic hardship and world wars, have a strong sense of personal privacy. They often approach digital technology with caution and are concerned about the security of their personal information online. Silents may be more inclined to use technology in a limited capacity, prioritising face-to-face communication and traditional forms of information exchange. They value personal privacy and may be hesitant to share personal information on social media or other online platforms.

Baby Boomers, who came of age during the cultural revolution of the 1960s and 1970s, have a diverse range of attitudes toward privacy and ethics in the digital age. While some Boomers are cautious about online privacy and the sharing of personal information, others have embraced social media and online interactions without significant privacy concerns. The ethical considerations for Boomers often revolve around issues of online etiquette, misinformation, and digital citizenship. They may be more aware of the potential consequences of their online behaviour and strive to maintain a sense of decorum in digital spaces.

Generation X, navigating the transition from analog to digital technologies, often approach privacy with a pragmatic mindset. They value their digital privacy but are willing to trade some personal information for convenience and personalised online experiences. Gen Xers are concerned about the security of their data and may take precautions such as using encryption and two-factor authentication. Ethical considerations for Gen X often centre around the responsible use of technology and the potential impact of their digital actions on others.

Millennials, raised in the information age, are particularly attuned to privacy and ethical considerations in the digital realm. They are concerned about the collection and use of their personal data by tech companies and social media platforms. Millennials have been vocal advocates for digital privacy rights and have pushed for transparency and accountability in the tech industry. Ethical considerations for Millennials include issues related to online harassment, cyberbullying, and the responsible use of social media.

Generation Z, the first true digital natives, have grown up in a world where privacy and ethical considerations are central to their online experiences. They are highly conscious of their digital footprint and the potential consequences of their online actions. Gen Zers are often advocates for digital privacy, cybersecurity, and ethical technology use. They are vocal about issues related to online misinformation, digital addiction, and the impact of technology on mental health.

The evolving landscape of privacy and ethical considerations is shaped by technological advancements, legislative changes, and societal attitudes. Each generation's approach to these issues reflects their unique experiences and perspectives. As we explore privacy and ethical considerations in the digital age, we gain insights into the ongoing dialogue about the responsible use of technology and the importance of protecting individual rights and values in the digital realm.

Chapter 6: The Generational Social Contract

Generational Perspectives on Social Welfare and Healthcare

The American social welfare system and healthcare landscape have evolved over the years, reflecting the values, priorities, and expectations of different generations. In this chapter, we'll explore the generational perspectives on social welfare and healthcare and how each generation has influenced and been influenced by these crucial aspects of society.

The Silent Generation, born during the Great Depression and World War II, experienced the early years of social welfare programs like Social Security and Medicare. They value the security and stability provided by these programs and are often concerned about their long-term sustainability. Silents appreciate the safety net these programs offer and are generally supportive of measures to protect and strengthen social welfare and healthcare systems.

Baby Boomers, who came of age during the postwar economic boom, have played a significant role in advocating for social justice and healthcare reform. They witnessed the civil rights movement and the push for universal healthcare coverage. Many Boomers have actively engaged in campaigns to expand access to healthcare services and reduce disparities. They place a high value on healthcare as a fundamental right and have supported policies aimed at achieving universal coverage.

Generation X, sandwiched between the idealism of the Boomers and the digital age, has navigated a changing landscape of social welfare and healthcare. They value individualism and self-reliance but also recognize the importance of safety nets. Gen Xers have often sought innovative solutions to address the challenges of healthcare access and affordability. They support policies that promote competition and consumer choice in healthcare while also emphasising the need for a robust safety net.

Millennials, raised in the digital age and coming of age during the Great Recession, have faced economic challenges and healthcare disparities. They are passionate advocates for healthcare reform and believe in the importance of universal coverage. Millennials have been instrumental in pushing for healthcare access through measures such as the Affordable Care Act (ACA). They also value mental health services and have been vocal about reducing the stigma surrounding mental health issues.

Generation Z, the first true digital natives, are entering adulthood with a focus on social justice and healthcare as human rights. They are concerned about the affordability and accessibility of healthcare services, especially as they face the transition to independent living and employment. Gen Zers are likely to continue advocating for healthcare reform and measures that address healthcare disparities. They also value holistic well-being, including mental health and preventive care.

Generational perspectives on social welfare and healthcare reflect a complex interplay of historical events, economic realities, and societal values. These perspectives influence the way each generation approaches issues such as healthcare reform, social safety nets, and the role of government in providing for the well-being of citizens. As we explore these perspectives, we gain insights into the ongoing dialogue about the future of social welfare and healthcare in America.

Education: A Lifelong Journey

Education is a cornerstone of personal and societal growth, and it plays a pivotal role in the lives of individuals across generations. In this chapter, we'll explore the evolving perspectives on education and the ways in which each generation has approached learning as a lifelong journey.

The Silent Generation, born during a time of economic hardship and world wars, often experienced limited educational opportunities compared to later generations. They value the importance of education and have seen the transformative power of knowledge in their own lives and communities. Silents have supported policies aimed at expanding access to education, particularly for disadvantaged populations. They believe that education is a key driver of social mobility and economic stability.

Baby Boomers, who came of age during the cultural revolution of the 1960s and 1970s, witnessed significant changes in the education system. They were among the first to experience the expansion of higher education opportunities, including the growth of colleges and universities. Boomers often view education as a path to personal growth and fulfilment. They have emphasised the importance of a college degree and have supported policies to make higher education more accessible, including federal financial aid programs.

Generation X, growing up in the 1980s and 1990s, navigated a changing educational landscape marked by budget constraints and shifting priorities. They saw the advent of standardised testing and the emphasis on academic performance. Gen Xers often approach education with a pragmatic mindset, valuing skills and practical knowledge. They have been advocates for vocational and technical education, recognizing the importance of preparing students for diverse career paths.

Millennials, raised in the information age, have faced the challenges of a competitive education system and the rising cost of higher education. They view education as a means to adapt to a rapidly changing job market. Many Millennials pursued higher education to secure better job opportunities, even as they grappled with student loan debt. They value lifelong learning and have embraced online education and skill-building platforms as a way to continuously update their knowledge and skills.

Generation Z, the first true digital natives, have grown up with a wealth of educational resources at their fingertips. They are comfortable with digital learning tools and value the flexibility and accessibility they offer. Gen Zers are likely to prioritise practical skills, entrepreneurship, and experiential learning. They are also advocates for educational equity and inclusivity, pushing for reforms that ensure all students have access to quality education regardless of their background.

The perspectives on education held by each generation reflect the evolving nature of learning in the modern world. Education is no longer confined to traditional classrooms but encompasses a lifelong journey of acquiring knowledge and skills. As we explore these generational perspectives on education, we gain insights into the changing landscape of learning and the ways in which different generations approach personal and professional development.

Retirement and Aging: Challenges and Solutions

The transition to retirement and the process of ageing are significant life stages that impact individuals and society as a whole. Each generation faces unique challenges and opportunities as they approach retirement age. In this chapter, we'll explore the generational perspectives on retirement and ageing, along with the solutions and strategies each generation employs to address these issues.

The Silent Generation, born during a time of economic hardship and world wars, often experienced traditional retirement at the age of 65. They value financial security and have generally followed a traditional retirement path, relying on pensions and Social Security. Silents have focused on saving for retirement and maintaining a sense of financial independence in their golden years. Many have embraced volunteerism and community involvement as a way to stay active and engaged in retirement.

Baby Boomers, who came of age during the postwar economic boom, have redefined retirement in many ways. They view retirement as an opportunity for personal growth and exploration. Many Boomers have delayed retirement to pursue second careers, start businesses, or engage in creative pursuits. They value active and healthy ageing and have embraced wellness and fitness as a way to maintain vitality in retirement. Additionally, Boomers are concerned about the financial challenges of retirement and are advocating for changes to Social Security and retirement savings policies.

Generation X, navigating the economic uncertainties of the late 20th century, approach retirement with a blend of pragmatism and adaptability. They recognize the importance of saving for retirement but often face challenges such as lower pension availability and the shifting landscape of retirement benefits. Gen Xers may prioritise work-life balance and plan for phased retirement, allowing them to gradually transition out of the workforce while pursuing personal interests and spending time with family.

Millennials, raised in the information age, have witnessed the financial struggles of earlier generations and are concerned about their own retirement prospects. They face the challenge of high student loan debt and the gig economy, which can make traditional retirement planning more difficult. Many Millennials are embracing a flexible approach to retirement, focusing on financial literacy and investment in assets like real estate. They are also advocates for policies that address retirement affordability and access to retirement plans.

Generation Z, the first true digital natives, are just beginning to consider retirement and ageing as long-term goals. They recognize the importance of financial literacy and are likely to prioritise saving for retirement from an early age. Gen Zers may approach retirement with a focus on sustainability and social impact, valuing investments that align with their values. They also place importance on maintaining work-life balance throughout their careers to ensure a fulfilling retirement.

The challenges and solutions related to retirement and ageing reflect the evolving expectations and values of each generation. As we explore these perspectives, we gain insights into the ways in which different generations are redefining the concept of retirement and seeking innovative solutions to ensure financial security and well-being in their later years.

Family Dynamics and Intergenerational Relationships

Family is the cornerstone of society, and the dynamics within families have evolved over generations, influenced by changing values, lifestyles, and societal norms. In this chapter, we'll explore how each generation approaches family dynamics and the intergenerational relationships that shape our lives.

The Silent Generation, born during a time of economic hardship and world wars, often experienced traditional family structures characterised by strong bonds and multigenerational households. They value family stability and have placed a premium on loyalty and commitment. Silents have a strong sense of duty toward their families, often providing care for their ageing parents and grandchildren. They prioritise face-to-face communication and have witnessed significant changes in family dynamics over their lifetimes.

Baby Boomers, who came of age during the cultural revolution of the 1960s and 1970s, challenged traditional family norms. They questioned authority and often pursued unconventional family arrangements. The Boomer generation witnessed the rise of divorce rates and the redefinition of gender roles within families. Many Boomers have sought to balance work and family life, striving for greater personal fulfilment. They value open communication and have played a pivotal role in shaping family dynamics in the modern era.

Generation X, growing up in the 1980s and 1990s, experienced the changing landscape of family dynamics firsthand. They often witnessed the challenges of dual-income households and the rise of single-parent families. Gen Xers place a strong emphasis on work-life balance and are known for their independence. They value quality time with their families and prioritise open and honest communication with their children. Gen X has also been instrumental in challenging traditional gender roles within families.

Millennials, raised in the information age, have faced unique family dynamics shaped by technological advancements and changing economic circumstances. They often grew up in dual-income households and have witnessed the impact of technology on family life, both positive and negative. Millennials value flexibility in their family arrangements, with many embracing non-traditional family structures, including cohabitation and non-marital partnerships. They are committed to maintaining strong relationships with their children and value open dialogue within their families.

Generation Z, the first true digital natives, are navigating family dynamics in a hyperconnected world. They are often characterised by close relationships with their parents and seek a balance between digital connectivity and face-to-face interactions within their families. Gen Zers value authenticity and open communication, and they are likely to challenge traditional family norms as they enter adulthood. They also place importance on diversity and inclusion within their families, valuing acceptance and support for all family members.

Intergenerational relationships within families are dynamic and continually evolving. Each generation brings its own values, expectations, and experiences to these relationships, influencing the way families interact and support one another. As we explore family dynamics and intergenerational relationships, we gain insights into the changing nature of family life in the modern era and the ways in which different generations navigate these important bonds.

Chapter 7: Bridging the Generational Divide

Strategies for Effective Communication Across Generations

Effective communication is the cornerstone of understanding and collaboration among generations. In this chapter, we'll explore strategies and best practices for bridging generational gaps and fostering positive interactions among individuals of all ages.

Active Listening: Regardless of generational background, active listening is a fundamental skill for effective communication. Encourage individuals to listen attentively to each other, ask clarifying questions, and seek to understand before being understood. Active listening fosters empathy and helps bridge generational gaps.

Flexibility and Adaptability: Recognize that different generations may have diverse communication styles and preferences. Be adaptable in your communication approach. For example, while younger generations may prefer digital communication, older generations might prefer face-to-face or phone conversations. Flexibility allows for more inclusive interactions.

Empathy: Cultivate empathy by understanding the perspectives, experiences, and values of individuals from different generations. Empathetic communication involves acknowledging the challenges and opportunities unique to each generation and showing respect for those differences.

Avoid Stereotyping: Stereotyping based on age can hinder effective communication. Avoid making assumptions or generalisations about individuals solely based on their generational cohort. Instead, treat each person as an individual with their own unique experiences and viewpoints.

Encourage Mentorship: Encourage intergenerational mentorship and knowledge sharing. Younger generations can learn valuable insights and wisdom from their older counterparts, while older generations can benefit from fresh perspectives and technological expertise. Mentorship programs can foster mutual respect and understanding.

Embrace Technology: Leverage technology to facilitate communication across generations. Encourage older generations to become familiar with digital communication tools, and younger generations to appreciate the value of in-person conversations. Finding a balance between digital and traditional communication can help bridge generational gaps.

Storytelling: Sharing personal stories and experiences can be a powerful way to connect across generations. Encourage individuals to share their life stories, lessons learned, and memorable moments. Storytelling helps create a sense of connection and understanding.

Respect Boundaries: Respect individual privacy and boundaries when communicating across generations. Avoid prying or intrusive questions and be mindful of personal preferences regarding sharing of information.

Appreciate Differences: Embrace generational differences as opportunities for growth and learning. Each generation brings its unique strengths and perspectives to the table. Recognize and appreciate these differences rather than seeing them as obstacles.

Foster Inclusivity: Create environments that promote inclusivity and respect for all generations. In workplaces, educational settings, and communities, ensure that policies and practices are designed to accommodate the needs and preferences of individuals from different age groups.

Seek Common Ground: Identify shared values and goals that transcend generational boundaries. Focusing on common ground can help unite generations in pursuing mutual objectives and collaborative efforts.

Lifelong Learning: Encourage a culture of lifelong learning among all generations. Learning from each other and staying open to new ideas and perspectives fosters continuous personal and professional growth.

Effective communication across generations is essential for building strong relationships, fostering collaboration, and addressing the complex challenges of our rapidly changing world. By employing these strategies, individuals and organisations can bridge generational gaps and create inclusive and harmonious environments that benefit everyone.

Building Bridges in the Workplace

In the modern workplace, where multiple generations often collaborate and share spaces, effective communication and collaboration are vital. Fostering intergenerational understanding and harmony in the workplace can lead to increased productivity, better teamwork, and a more inclusive work environment. In this chapter, we'll explore strategies for building bridges and promoting synergy among different generations in the workplace.

Generational Awareness Training: Employers can offer generational awareness training to employees. This training can help individuals understand the characteristics, values, and communication styles of different generations. By increasing awareness, employees can be more empathetic and adaptable in their interactions.

Mentorship Programs: Implement mentorship programs that encourage employees from different generations to connect and learn from each other. Younger employees can benefit from the wisdom and experience of older colleagues, while older employees can gain fresh perspectives from their younger counterparts.

Cross-Generational Teams: Form cross-generational teams for projects and assignments. Encourage collaboration and idea sharing among team members of different age groups. Diverse teams often produce more innovative and well-rounded solutions.

Flexible Work Arrangements: Offer flexible work arrangements, such as remote work options or flexible hours, to accommodate the diverse needs and preferences of different generations. Flexibility can improve work-life balance and job satisfaction.

Communication Channels: Provide multiple communication channels that cater to different generational preferences. While younger employees may prefer digital communication, older employees might favour in-person meetings or phone calls. Ensuring diverse communication options can facilitate better information flow.

Reverse Mentoring: Implement reverse mentoring programs where younger employees mentor older employees in areas like technology and digital trends. This not only enhances digital literacy among older employees but also fosters intergenerational relationships.

Inclusive Decision-Making: Encourage inclusive decision-making processes where employees from various generations have the opportunity to contribute ideas and feedback. Make sure that all voices are heard and valued during discussions.

Continuous Learning: Promote a culture of continuous learning and skill development for all employees. Encourage older employees to embrace new technologies and younger employees to tap into the knowledge of older colleagues.

Recognize Generational Contributions: Recognize and celebrate the unique contributions of each generation in the workplace. Highlight the strengths and talents that individuals from different age groups bring to the team.

Conflict Resolution: Develop effective conflict resolution mechanisms that address generational conflicts or misunderstandings promptly and professionally. Encourage open dialogue and mediation when necessary.

Organisational Values: Define and communicate the core values and goals of the organisation. Align these values with the generational values and aspirations of employees. A shared sense of purpose can bridge generational divides.

Feedback Culture: Foster a feedback culture where employees are encouraged to provide constructive feedback on workplace practices, including those related to generational interactions. Use feedback to continuously improve the work environment.

Building bridges in the workplace requires a proactive and inclusive approach. By recognizing and leveraging the strengths of each generation and fostering an environment of mutual respect, organisations can harness the full potential of a multigenerational workforce. This not only benefits individual employees but also contributes to the overall success and innovation of the organisation.

Fostering Generational Understanding in Families and Communities

The need for generational understanding extends beyond the workplace; it also plays a crucial role in families and communities. Strengthening intergenerational relationships can promote harmony, shared values, and a sense of belonging among individuals of all ages. In this chapter, we'll explore strategies for fostering generational understanding in families and communities.

Open and Inclusive Conversations: Encourage open and inclusive conversations within families and communities. Create spaces where individuals of all generations feel comfortable expressing their thoughts, concerns, and aspirations. These conversations can occur during family gatherings, community meetings, or support groups.

Intergenerational Activities: Organise intergenerational activities that bring different generations together. These activities can include family game nights, community service projects, or workshops. Shared experiences foster connections and understanding.

Storytelling and Oral History: Embrace the tradition of storytelling and oral history within families and communities. Encourage older generations to share their life stories, experiences, and wisdom with younger members. These stories provide valuable insights into the past and foster a sense of continuity.

Volunteerism: Promote intergenerational volunteerism. Encourage family members and community residents of all ages to engage in volunteer activities together. This not only benefits the community but also strengthens bonds across generations.

Celebrate Milestones: Celebrate generational milestones and achievements. Whether it's a high school graduation, a retirement party, or a 50th wedding anniversary, acknowledging and celebrating these milestones brings generations together in meaningful ways.

Family and Community Traditions: Emphasise the importance of family and community traditions. Traditions provide a sense of continuity and shared identity. Involve multiple generations in the planning and continuation of these traditions.

Educational Programs: Offer educational programs and workshops on generational understanding. These programs can be held in schools, community centres, or religious institutions. They provide opportunities for individuals to learn about the experiences and perspectives of different generations.

Intergenerational Support Networks: Establish intergenerational support networks where individuals of different generations can seek guidance, mentorship, and assistance. These networks can address a wide range of needs, from career advice to emotional support.

Empathy-Building Exercises: Develop empathy-building exercises that encourage individuals to step into the shoes of someone from a different generation. This can include role-playing scenarios or guided discussions that explore generational challenges and experiences.

Respect for Diversity: Emphasise the importance of respecting generational diversity within families and communities. Encourage individuals to appreciate the unique qualities and contributions of each generation.

Intergenerational Housing: Consider intergenerational housing arrangements where multiple generations live together or in close proximity. These arrangements can provide mutual support and foster generational understanding.

Generational Committees: Establish generational committees or advisory groups within communities or organisations. These committees can provide input and recommendations on policies and programs that affect different age groups.

Fostering generational understanding in families and communities is a collaborative effort that benefits everyone involved. By recognizing the value of diverse generational perspectives and actively working to bridge generational gaps, families and communities can create environments where individuals of all ages feel respected, valued, and connected. This sense of unity contributes to the overall well-being and vibrancy of families and communities.

The Power of Collaboration

Collaboration across generations holds immense potential for addressing the complex challenges of our rapidly changing world. When individuals from different age groups come together to share their perspectives, insights, and skills, they can create innovative solutions and drive positive change in families, communities, workplaces, and society at large. In this chapter, we'll explore the transformative power of collaboration across generations.

Diverse Perspectives: Collaboration across generations brings together diverse perspectives and experiences. Younger generations often offer fresh insights and technological expertise, while older generations provide wisdom, historical context, and practical know-how. Combining these perspectives can lead to more comprehensive and effective solutions.

Enhanced Problem Solving: When individuals of different generations collaborate, they can tackle complex problems with a broader range of solutions. Older generations may have encountered similar challenges in the past, offering tried-and-true approaches, while younger generations may introduce innovative, tech-savvy solutions.

Mentorship and Learning: Collaborative efforts enable mentorship and learning opportunities. Younger individuals can learn from the experiences of their older counterparts, while older individuals can stay updated on new technologies and trends. This exchange of knowledge is mutually beneficial.

Bridging Digital Divides: Collaboration across generations helps bridge digital divides. Younger generations can assist older ones in becoming more digitally literate, while older generations can offer insights into managing digital information responsibly.

Fostering Empathy: Collaborative projects encourage empathy and understanding among generations. Working together allows individuals to see the world through each other's eyes, fostering a sense of connection and shared purpose.

Innovation and Creativity: Diverse generational perspectives stimulate innovation and creativity. The combination of traditional wisdom and contemporary thinking often results in groundbreaking ideas and approaches.

Community Building: Collaborative efforts strengthen communities by reinforcing bonds between generations. This sense of community can enhance social cohesion and create a supportive environment for all residents.

Personal Growth: Collaborative experiences promote personal growth and development. Individuals from different generations can challenge each other to expand their horizons, acquire new skills, and become more adaptable.

Overcoming Stereotypes: Collaboration helps overcome generational stereotypes and biases. Interacting on equal footing dispels myths and misconceptions, leading to more respectful and inclusive relationships.

Social Impact: Collaborative initiatives can have a profound social impact. When generations work together to address pressing issues, such as climate change, poverty, or healthcare access, they have the potential to drive positive change on a large scale.

Legacy Building: Collaborative efforts enable the creation of lasting legacies. By passing down knowledge, values, and traditions from one generation to the next, families and communities can preserve their unique identities and cultural heritage.

Collective Wisdom: Collaboration across generations harnesses collective wisdom. It acknowledges that each generation has something valuable to offer and that by working together, we can build a stronger, more resilient society.

The power of collaboration across generations lies in its ability to transcend differences and create synergistic relationships that benefit everyone involved. By embracing collaboration as a guiding principle, we can unlock the full potential of a multigenerational world and work together to shape a brighter future for all.

Chapter 8: Shaping America's Future

The Intersection of Generations and Policy

Public policy serves as a powerful instrument that shapes the lives, experiences, and opportunities of individuals at different stages of life. It is the arena where the needs and aspirations of various generations converge and find expression. In this chapter, we embark on a journey to explore the profound impact of policy across generations, delving into areas such as education, healthcare, social welfare, employment, housing, technology, and environmental concerns.

Education Policy: Education policies stand as pillars upon which younger generations build their futures. They define the quality and accessibility of educational opportunities, from early childhood programs to higher education. By ensuring affordable and accessible education, policymakers empower individuals to equip themselves with the skills and knowledge needed to thrive in an ever-evolving world.

Healthcare Policy: Healthcare policies weave the fabric of well-being that touches individuals of all ages. These policies encompass access to quality healthcare, affordability of insurance options, and the promotion of preventative care measures. The intersection of generational needs becomes particularly pronounced in healthcare policy, where it addresses the diverse healthcare requirements of individuals across their lifespans.

Social Welfare Policy: Social welfare policies form a vital safety net for older generations, providing critical support during retirement and later stages of life. Policymakers face the monumental challenge of ensuring the sustainability of programs such as Social Security and Medicare while adapting to the evolving needs of an ageing population.

Employment and Labor Policy: Employment and labour policies lay the groundwork for the workforce, affecting individuals of all ages. These policies encompass issues such as minimum wage, workplace safety standards, anti-discrimination measures, and retirement benefits. They wield a substantial influence over the economic security and opportunities available to individuals across the generational spectrum.

Housing Policy: Housing policies have a far-reaching impact, touching individuals of all ages. These policies address the complexities of housing affordability, accessibility, and inclusivity. Policymakers grapple with the challenge of providing affordable housing for young adults while also considering the housing needs of older generations seeking age-appropriate accommodations.

Technology and Digital Policy: In the digital age, technology and digital policies have emerged at the forefront of policy making. These policies tackle pressing issues such as digital privacy, internet accessibility, and cybersecurity. They are essential for safeguarding individuals from diverse age groups in an increasingly interconnected world.

Environmental Policy: Environmental policies are paramount for securing the well-being of current and future generations. They address critical concerns such as climate change, conservation of natural resources, and the adoption of sustainable practices. These policies necessitate collective action and transcend generational boundaries in their significance.

Navigating the intricate web of public policy unveils how these regulations, meticulously crafted to address the intricate needs and aspirations of individuals spanning the generational spectrum, serve as a foundational backdrop against which the generations coexist, interact, and collectively shape the future of our society. Understanding the intersection of generations and policy is essential for creating a harmonious and equitable society that accommodates the diverse needs and aspirations of all its members.

Opportunities for Unity and Innovation

In our exploration of the intersection between generations and policy, we uncover significant opportunities for unity and innovation. This chapter delves into how the generational landscape, when thoughtfully considered in policy making, can lead to collaboration, synergy, and transformative progress.

Cross-Generational Collaboration: Policymakers have a unique opportunity to foster cross-generational collaboration. By bringing together individuals from different age groups in the policy development process, we can harness the collective wisdom, experiences, and fresh perspectives of each generation. This collaborative approach often results in innovative solutions that address the multifaceted needs of society.

Intergenerational Mentorship: Policies can encourage and support intergenerational mentorship initiatives. These programs create bridges between older and younger generations, allowing the transfer of knowledge, skills, and insights. Such mentorship relationships enhance personal development and professional growth while bridging generational divides.

Innovation in Education: Education policies hold immense potential for innovation. Policymakers can explore novel approaches to education, integrating modern technology, personalised learning, and lifelong education. These innovations ensure that education remains relevant and adaptable to the evolving needs of each generation.

Healthcare Advancements: Policies can drive healthcare advancements that benefit individuals of all ages. Investments in medical research, preventive care, and telemedicine can improve healthcare access and quality, promoting healthier, more fulfilling lives for everyone.

Social Welfare Reinvention: Social welfare policies can undergo a process of reinvention to better align with changing demographics and societal needs. Policymakers can explore flexible retirement options, affordable eldercare solutions, and innovative approaches to address poverty and social inequality.

Workforce Adaptation: Employment policies can adapt to the evolving workforce. Policies supporting lifelong learning, remote work options, and age-inclusive practices can empower individuals to remain active contributors to the workforce throughout their lives.

Technological Innovation: Digital policies can encourage technological innovation that benefits all generations. Policymakers can support initiatives that bridge the digital divide, protect digital privacy, and promote ethical tech practices, ensuring that technology is a force for inclusivity and progress.

Environmental Stewardship: Environmental policies offer an opportunity for collective action. Policies aimed at addressing climate change, conserving natural resources, and promoting sustainability are essential for safeguarding the planet for current and future generations.

As we navigate the complex landscape of generational diversity, these opportunities for unity and innovation serve as beacons of hope. Policymakers and society at large can harness the strengths and insights of each generation, working together to build a brighter future that embraces the needs and aspirations of all its members.

Preparing for the Next Generational Wave

In our exploration of the interplay between generations and policy, it becomes evident that our society is in a constant state of flux. The generational dynamics shaping our world today will continue to evolve, and policymakers must proactively prepare for the waves of generations that lie ahead. This chapter delves into the forward-thinking strategies essential for navigating the ever-changing generational landscape.

Anticipating Emerging Needs: Policymakers must maintain a forward-looking perspective, anticipating the emerging needs of future generations. This involves staying attuned to demographic shifts, technological advancements, and evolving societal values. By doing so, we can craft policies that are responsive and adaptable to the unique challenges and opportunities that lie ahead.

Flexible Policy Frameworks: In an era of rapid change, rigid policies may quickly become obsolete. Policymakers should consider implementing flexible policy frameworks that can be adjusted and refined as new generational dynamics emerge. This flexibility ensures that policies remain effective and relevant over time.

Intergenerational Equity: Embracing intergenerational equity as a guiding principle can help policymakers make decisions that balance the needs of different generations. This approach involves considering the long-term consequences of policies on future generations and making choices that promote fairness and sustainability.

Embracing Technological Advancements: Technology will continue to be a driving force in generational change. Policymakers should embrace technological advancements and foster an environment where innovation is encouraged. This includes investing in digital infrastructure, promoting digital literacy, and addressing potential ethical and privacy concerns.

Continued Dialogue: To prepare for the next generational wave, policymakers must maintain open and continued dialogue with individuals from all age groups. This ensures that policies are informed by the diverse perspectives and insights of the population, making them more inclusive and effective.

Adaptive Social Welfare: Social welfare policies should evolve to accommodate the changing needs of generations. Policymakers should consider innovative approaches to address challenges such as retirement security, healthcare, and social safety nets while ensuring these systems remain sustainable for future generations.

Education for Lifelong Learning: Education policies should prioritise lifelong learning. Preparing individuals to adapt to a rapidly changing world requires a commitment to ongoing education and skills development throughout life. Policymakers can support initiatives that promote accessible and relevant educational opportunities for all generations.

As we peer into the horizon of generational change, these forward-thinking strategies serve as a compass guiding policy makers toward policies that are not only responsive to the current generation but also well-prepared to welcome and embrace the generations of tomorrow. In doing so, we ensure a society that continues to evolve, innovate, and thrive, honouring the unique qualities and aspirations of each generation.

The Vision for America's Future

As we conclude our exploration of the intricate relationship between generations and policy, we cast our gaze toward a vision for America's future. In this chapter, we paint a picture of a society that thrives on intergenerational cooperation, equity, and innovation—a society that honours the past, embraces the present, and welcomes the generations yet to come.

Unity Across Generations: The vision for America's future envisions a society where unity across generations is not just an ideal but a reality. It's a place where generational divides are bridged, where the wisdom of elders is celebrated, and the fresh perspectives of the young are valued. It's a society where every generation contributes to the betterment of the whole.

Equity and Inclusivity: In this vision, equity and inclusivity are the cornerstones of policymaking. It's a society where policies are designed to ensure that every individual, regardless of age, gender, race, or background, has equal access to opportunities, resources, and a fulfilling life. It's a place where intergenerational fairness is upheld, and the burdens and benefits of policies are shared equitably.

Innovation and Adaptability: The vision for America's future embraces innovation and adaptability. It's a society where policies are agile, capable of responding swiftly to the ever-changing needs and challenges posed by new generations. It's a place where technological advancements are harnessed to improve lives, where education continually evolves, and where healthcare is accessible to all.

Sustainability and Responsibility: Sustainability and responsibility are fundamental principles in this vision. It's a society that takes its environmental responsibilities seriously, recognizing that we are stewards of the planet for future generations. It's a place where economic, social, and environmental policies are designed with the long-term well-being of all generations in mind.

A Lifelong Learning Culture: The vision fosters a lifelong learning culture. It's a society where education doesn't end with a diploma but continues throughout life. It's a place where individuals are encouraged to adapt, acquire new skills, and remain engaged in their communities and workplaces well into their later years.

Interconnected Communities: In this vision, communities are interconnected and supportive. It's a society where neighbours of all ages come together to address common challenges and celebrate shared successes. It's a place where generations live in harmony, where the elderly are not isolated, and the young are not marginalised.

A Legacy of Resilience: The vision for America's future cherishes a legacy of resilience. It's a society that draws strength from the struggles and triumphs of past generations. It's a place where the lessons of history are learned and applied to face contemporary and future challenges with courage and determination.

Empowerment of Future Leaders: Lastly, this vision empowers future leaders. It's a society where the next generation is nurtured, encouraged, and equipped with the skills and knowledge to become compassionate and capable leaders. It's a place where leadership is not defined by age but by merit and vision.

As we chart the course for America's future, this vision serves as a guiding star—a reminder that the generational shifts we experience are not disruptions but opportunities for growth, adaptation, and progress. By embracing this vision, we can create a society that thrives on the unique contributions of each generation and welcomes a future that is brighter, more inclusive, and more promising than ever before.

Conclusion: Decoding the Tapestry of America's Generations

Reflections on the Generational Journey

As we conclude our journey through the generational tapestry of America, it's essential to pause and reflect on the insights we've gathered along the way. Our exploration has taken us on a voyage through the lives, experiences, and evolving roles of the Silent Generation, Baby Boomers, Generation X, Millennials, and Generation Z. We've navigated the complexities of their worldviews, their contributions to society, and the profound impact of generational shifts on our nation's past, present, and future.

In these reflections, we find several key themes that have emerged throughout our exploration:

1. **Interconnectedness**: One striking revelation is the interconnectedness of generations. Despite their differences, each generation has played a pivotal role in shaping the trajectory of American history. They are not isolated entities but threads woven into the intricate tapestry of our nation's story.

2. **Adaptation**: Another theme that emerges is the remarkable adaptability of generations. They have faced a changing world with resilience, each generation finding its own unique way to navigate the challenges of their time. From the Silent Generation's post-war rebuilding to Generation Z's digital fluency, adaptability has been a constant.

3. **Shared Values**: While each generation brings its unique values and priorities, there is a thread of shared values that transcends generational lines. The desire for a better future, a sense of community, and the pursuit of happiness are ideals that have remained steadfast across the generations.

4. Generational Diversity: Our exploration underscores the richness of generational diversity. It's a reminder that a diverse society is a strong society, and by embracing the perspectives and experiences of different generations, we enrich our collective wisdom and potential.

5. Collaboration and Innovation: The stories of generations collaborating and innovating together stand out as beacons of hope. Whether it's the mentorship between generations, the synergy of intergenerational workplaces, or the collective effort to address societal challenges, collaboration and innovation are powerful forces for progress.

6. Challenges and Solutions: We've also encountered the challenges faced by each generation—economic hardships, social upheaval, technological disruption, and environmental concerns. But with these challenges come opportunities for growth, resilience, and solutions that can benefit all.

7. A Multigenerational Vision: Ultimately, our journey leaves us with a vision of a multigenerational society—a society where the strengths of each generation are harnessed to create a brighter future. It's a vision of a society that values wisdom and innovation, empathy and ambition, continuity and change.

In closing, our exploration of America's generations has been a voyage of discovery and understanding. It is a testament to the ever-evolving nature of our society, a reminder of the richness that generational diversity brings, and an invitation to embrace the future with optimism and unity. The generations of America are not separate entities; they are chapters in a collective story, each contributing to the rich tapestry of our nation's history.

The Ongoing Evolution of American Society

As we stand at the crossroads of generational change, it's essential to recognize that the evolution of American society is a perpetual journey. The generations we've explored in this book have shaped the nation in profound ways, and as we move forward, we must acknowledge that this journey continues.

Our society is not static but dynamic, and each generation plays a unique role in the ongoing narrative of America. The challenges and opportunities that lie ahead require us to adapt, collaborate, and innovate as we have done in the past. We must embrace the idea that the evolution of American society is a collective endeavour that transcends generational boundaries.

In the spirit of intergenerational cooperation, we can harness the strengths of each generation to address the pressing issues of our time—from climate change and technological transformation to social equity and global connectivity. By working together, we can ensure that the America of tomorrow is a place where all generations thrive, where wisdom is honoured, and where progress is a shared pursuit.

The Collective Responsibility to Shape Tomorrow

The generational journey we've embarked upon is not just a matter of understanding the past and present; it's a call to action for the future. As we conclude this exploration, we must recognize our collective responsibility to shape tomorrow.

Each generation has a role to play in shaping the world that future generations will inherit. It's a responsibility to leave a legacy of resilience, compassion, and progress. It's a call to prioritise sustainability, equity, and inclusivity in our actions and policies.

In this collective endeavour, we must acknowledge that the challenges and opportunities of our time are not isolated to a single generation. They are shared by all, and the solutions require the contributions of each generation. Together, we can forge a path forward that honours the past, engages with the present, and welcomes the generations yet to come.

The future of America is not predetermined; it is a canvas waiting for the brushstrokes of generations to come. It is a story waiting to be written by the hands of those who understand the value of intergenerational cooperation and the power of unity.

As we conclude our generational journey, let us carry forward the insights, lessons, and visions we've uncovered. Let us embrace the ongoing evolution of American society with hope, determination, and a commitment to leaving a positive mark on the world.

Thank you for joining us on this journey through the generations of America. May our collective efforts continue to shape a future that reflects the best qualities of each generation and the enduring spirit of our nation.

Appendix B: Resources for Further Reading

Books, Articles, and Websites on Generational Studies

1. **"Generations: The History of America's Future, 1584 to 2069"** by William Strauss and Neil Howe - This seminal work provides a comprehensive analysis of generational theory and its impact on American history.

2. **"The Fourth Turning: An American Prophecy"** by William Strauss and Neil Howe - Delve deeper into generational cycles and their implications for the future of America.

3. **"Generations at Work: Managing the Clash of Veterans, Boomers, Xers, and Nexters in Your Workplace"** by Ron Zemke, Claire Raines, and Bob Filipczak - A practical guide to understanding and managing generational differences in the workplace.

4. **"The Defining Decade: Why Your Twenties Matter and How to Make the Most of Them Now"** by Meg Jay - Explores the challenges and opportunities facing Millennials as they navigate the transition to adulthood.

5. **"iGen: Why Today's Super-Connected Kids Are Growing Up Less Rebellious, More Tolerant, Less Happy—and Completely Unprepared for Adulthood"** by Jean M. Twenge - A deep dive into the characteristics and experiences of Generation Z.

6. **"The Age of Surveillance Capitalism: The Fight for a Human Future at the New Frontier of Power"** by Shoshana Zuboff - An exploration of the impact of technology on society, particularly relevant for understanding how it has shaped recent generations.

7. **"Generation Me: Why Today's Young Americans Are More Confident, Assertive, Entitled—and More Miserable Than Ever Before"** by Jean M. Twenge - Examines the traits and challenges of Millennials.

8. **"Gen Z @ Work: How the Next Generation Is Transforming the Workplace"** by David Stillman and Jonah Stillman - An insightful look into Generation Z's entry into the workforce.

9. **"Boomer Nation: The Largest and Richest Generation Ever, and How It Changed America"** by Steve Gillon - An exploration of the Baby Boomer generation's impact on American society.

10. **"The Silents: Silent Heroes"** by Gerard J. De Groot - A historical perspective on the Silent Generation and their contributions to post-war America.

11. **"Generations, Inc.: From Boomers to Linksters—Managing the Friction Between Generations at Work"** by Meagan Johnson and Larry Johnson - Offers practical advice for creating productive multigenerational workplaces.

12. **"The Longevity Economy: Unlocking the World's Fastest-Growing, Most Misunderstood Market"** by Joseph F. Coughlin - Explores the economic and social implications of an ageing population.

13. **"The Power of Moments: Why Certain Experiences Have Extraordinary Impact"** by Chip Heath and Dan Heath - Offers insights into creating meaningful intergenerational moments.

Including these resources for further reading at the end of your book will provide readers with opportunities to delve deeper into the fascinating world of generational studies and related topics.

Acknowledgments

Gratitude to Those Who Contributed to the Book

As I pen these words, I am acutely aware that no book is the sole creation of its author. It is a collective effort, a tapestry woven from the threads of knowledge, support, and inspiration provided by countless individuals. To each of you who contributed to the making of this book, I extend my heartfelt gratitude.

To My Family: You have been my steadfast pillars of support, providing encouragement, patience, and understanding throughout this journey. Your unwavering belief in me has been my greatest motivation.

To My Editor and Publishing Team: A special thanks to my dedicated editor and the entire publishing team who worked tirelessly to bring this book to life. Your expertise and guidance have been invaluable.

To the Generational Experts: To the researchers, scholars, and experts in the field of generational studies, thank you for your groundbreaking research and insights. Your work has laid the foundation for this exploration.

To the Interviewees: To those who graciously shared their generational experiences and stories, thank you for providing a human dimension to this book. Your voices have enriched its narrative.

To My Mentors: I am grateful for the wisdom and mentorship provided by those who have guided my understanding of generational dynamics and the intricacies of storytelling.

To the Readers: To all who pick up this book, I am honoured by your interest. It is your curiosity and engagement that give purpose to these pages.

To the Generations: To the Silent Generation, Baby Boomers, Generation X, Millennials, Generation Z, and Generation Alpha—your collective experiences are the heartbeat of this book. It is a tribute to the tapestry you have collectively woven.

This book is a product of collaboration, learning, and the belief that understanding our generational differences is a path to greater unity. It is a testament to the power of storytelling and the resilience of the American spirit.

In closing, thank you all for being a part of this endeavour. May the pages ahead be both enlightening and thought-provoking, sparking conversations and fostering a deeper understanding of the generations that shape our world.

With heartfelt gratitude,

Ethan Winters

About the Author

A Brief Biography of Ethan Winters

Dear Reader,

Let me begin by saying that writing this book has been an extraordinary adventure for me—a journey I embarked upon without formal writing training but with a heart full of passion and a curious spirit. I'm Ethan Winters, and "From Boom to Zoom: Decoding America's Generational Shift" marks my very first foray into the world of authorship.

My path to writing this book was unconventional, driven not by academic pursuits but by a deep fascination with stories and a burning desire to understand the generations that shape our world. I don't hold a degree in writing or literature; instead, my background is rooted in a different field altogether. But that's what makes this journey all the more special—it's a testament to the power of curiosity and the determination to explore uncharted territory.

Generational dynamics have always intrigued me, and as I delved deeper into this subject, I found myself uncovering layers of complexity and nuance that begged to be shared. This book is the result of countless hours of research, late nights wrestling with words, and the unwavering belief that the stories of generations are a tapestry worth unravelling.

Beyond the pages of this book, you'll find me immersed in nature, seeking solace and inspiration in its beauty. I'm a firm believer in the lessons nature teaches us about balance, resilience, and the interconnectedness of life—lessons that have shaped my perspective on generational harmony.

As a first-time author, I've poured my heart and soul into this project, not as an expert in writing but as a passionate storyteller. My hope is that my genuine curiosity and dedication shine through in these pages, making the journey of discovery enjoyable and relatable for you, the reader.

"From Boom to Zoom" is not just a book; it's an invitation to join me on a personal odyssey through the generations. It's a celebration of the stories that define us, connect us, and help us make sense of our world. It's a reminder that every one of us has a unique story to tell, regardless of our background or training.

Thank you for taking this journey with me, a journey that I've embarked upon with both excitement and humility. I look forward to sharing the stories of America's Silent Generation, Baby Boomers, Generation X, Millennials, Generation Z, and Generation Alpha with you, and I hope that together, we'll uncover the threads that weave our shared history.

Warmly,

Ethan Winters